Johan Isaac Hollandus

Opuscula Alchimica

The Art of Alchemy consists in three things, that is, in our Stone. That is, the free art of the ancients and their successors who are to discover this free art through Science or Practice; or to whomever the Holy Ghost gives it, or upon who He confers it through His illumination; and blessed is he who possesses this free art and applies it wisely for the honor of God and the pressing need of his fellow man.

The other kind of alchemy is the Elixir which is prepared, as the ancients taught, according to the hand of the Philosophers. Those who have this and understand it well may also be called blessed.

The third kind is the Ixir, and it is also an art of the old and wise masters of the hand, and he who knows how to prepare it, as the fathers prepared it and have left it to us, will likewise rule in this world of joys.

The Art of Alchemy has still many more daughters, branches and roots which spring from these three trees of which I have just spoken, such as: Some labor with hard work in the Calcination of the bodies, to wash them and make them pure and clean. Others labor with amalgamationibus: others with albination, cementation, augmentation and rubifacation. Others make Salia of the bodies or the metals. Others make Olea and other works of the bodies in the fire. Others with Aquis fortibus, others of the bodies in the fire. Others with Aquis fortibus, others with salia upon the corpora; and so on, in many different ways. And everything is good if it is done in the right way as the forefathers have taught; but all this is attained only through great effort.

If then someone has married one of these daughters, he will never again be in want, but it has to be achieved by dint of great effort and care; and it would really be necessary for a good and experienced alchemist to have all these daughters in marriage, to know well and understand all these operations, to enable to distinguish between good and bad; but enough of this.

Now to revert to our thema, that is, to our Stone of the free art. Open your ears, then, and see; open your understanding and take note, for I will reveal to most secret matters which no one has as yet revealed. I will disclose more to you than I have been told to. If you have the least bit of intelligence, you will understand it, as otherwise God will not give it to you.

Listen: Before our Stone has become sufficient, it is already alive! And when it is found, it is dead! Moreover, everyone sees it and holds his nose before the Materi.

The Stone Of Urine

A Good and Sincere Work of Isaac Hollandus

Before our Stone comes into existence, it is alive; when it is found, it is dead; everyone sees it and hold his nose before it. It had lain on top of the casks or vessels in which it was kept, for a long time, and one and all hold their noses before the Materi or stinking air from which our Stone is drawn. The poor have it as well as the rich; little children as well as older people. It is indeed, a child's play and a woman's work, and the ignorant people have diligently searched for it, long and hard, in excrements and have not found it. For when you are alive, the Stone lives with you. That is the reason why one cannot draw our Stone out of excrements, since our Stone possesses the four elements perfectly; yes, it is more wonderful than anyting on earth. For man is the very best, which God has created in this world in his image. If you have some intelligence, listen.

Our stone has a strong smell and bitter taste, like urine, and it is found everywhere in superfluous quantity. All animals also have it, though not as perfectly as man. Without our Stone nothing in this world can live. I am telling you enough, if will only understand; and if you do not understand, God Almighty will not grant it to you; and even if you do not find it, it is nevertheless found.

Our Stone is in all things that grow out of the earth, and it is also in the earth, likewise in ditches and also above the earth. Should God then provide that you may find it and know its nature, we will inform you how to extract it and how to proceed in order to draw the Stone of it, of what color it is, what it must look like when it has been made; likewise how to handle it to prepare it.

Item, our Stone costs little and can easily be found everywhere, in all street corners, in all secret chambers; on dung heaps and in caverns and vaults or in stables, there is an abundance of it. It grows and greens in all places where its water is found and where it lies quietly. Our Stone also grows out of the foul, stinking Materi in which it is white and clear, just as glass grows out of the foul earth and is also beautiful and clear. Therefore the ancients and wise men write: Our Stone purified itself and separates itself from all uncleanliness. The ignorant ones, who do not understand this, rebuke the ancients for having said this, and believe that it is mercury. And further, our Stone rises above all Faeces and ascends up high, where it collects.

Item, if you know the Stone, take it in its coarseness, congeal it till it is thick, and guard it from all metals, because the Stone would turn into weeds, for it is their nature to make all things pure and clean. When you have made it thick or have congealed it, you may draw from it the two elements air and fire. The third element, earth, lies burnt black, like coal, in fundo of the vessel, In the black coal there is hidden the Stone of the old and wise philosophers as also of the sworn Masters. Pulverize this black earth intangibly. Put it into a wide vessel in tripode to calcinate for four days, glowing in moderate heat, so that the matter stands between glowing and not glowing. But the last day, let it glow nicely, but not too much, as the matter must not melt; for as long as our Stone is not pure, it is combustible, and the Stone together with the foul Materi would burn to glass if the Materi were to reach the melting stage. That is why the ancients forbid heating with the Spirit and the soul; for the Spiritus preserves the Corpus, so that the fire cannot either burn it or harm it; and the pure, clear corpus protects the spiritus, so that it stays in the fire and does not fly away while the body is fixed; and this it does not let it fly away from it. The spiritus is incombustible. That is why the spiritus does not allow the corpus to burn, for they are one by means of the spiritus and the soul on the spiritus and with the body. For although a pure spiritus and corpus are joined together, the fire would nevertheless separate body and spirit, and the spirit would escape. But when the soul is joined to the body together with the spirit, and they are all pure, they are one. Then neither fire or water nor anything in the world can destroy them, for it is a perfect thing.

Item, when the earth is thus calcinated, take it out of tripode and dissolve it in common, distilled water; let the faeces drop, and as long as it is still warm pour the water above off into a wooden or stone vessel. Do be on guard against the metals, otherwise the blessed Stone will be spoiled and corrupted. Now the blessed Stone will sprout beautifully and purely, and grow like grass out of the earth, ever more and more.

Now pour the water of the sprouted matter into a stone vessel which must not be coated with lead, or into a glass vessel. Boil the water, and again pour it into a wooden or stone vessel. let it sprout again, and each time something has sprouted, boil the water down till everything has sprouted.

When everything has been boiled down and has sprouted, dry it over a gentle fire, stirring with a fine rod till the matter is so dry that it dusts. Now put the matter into a wide vessel, of one thumb's thickness, and set it in tripode or a reverberating furnace. This is the best and last calcinations, which is to last three hours; the first hour with a gentle fire, the second with a stronger fire, and the third hour the fire must be heated so strongly that it reaches the stage between glowing and not glowing. Toward the end of the last hour increase the fire so much that the matter glows nicely without melting. If you see it melt, remove the fire from the furnace as fast as you can, and let the matter cool down.

Now take it out and dissolve it in pure water. When it has settled, pour the pure off from its sediment while it is warm; for if you allowed it to grow cold, the Stone would crystallize of its own, and you would be unable to clarify it of its faecibus. You must do this --- dissolve in water, pour off its sediemtn and allow itto sprout, and pour it off again, and boil it down, and let it sprout again --- till everything is sprouted.

Then you must again dry the matter over a gentle fire, always stirring it with a little rod till it dusts, as mentioned before! Now put it back into the wide vessel of one thumb's thickness and into a reverberating furnace, till your Stone no longer gives off any faeces and stay clear and subtle, and melts on a hot tin like wax or butter. F it is taken off the fire, it must stand up and not dissolve even in cold and humid air. Then your Stone is subtle and fixed.

But if it should happen that the Stone should melt during calcinations, it would not be spoiled because of it, but you would lose your weight; for if the Stone were standing long enough in flux in the fire, part of it would burn into glass, for the Stone is still alone and at that time does not yet have its spiritus with it, which could protect the corpus from the fire. Likewise, it does not have the soul with it, which would keep the spiritus and the corpus together in peace. When, however, spirit, body, and soul are united together, fire cannot turn them into glass, for it is then an elixir that surpasses all elixirs. Then it is a glorified corpus which is perfect. Then it is the indestructible corpus which is perfect. Then it is the indestructible Quintessence, similar to the unconquerable heaven. And when you have thus prepared it, the Stone desires to receive the spirit and the soul. When you have got it to this stage, you have accomplished all that the ancients expounded covertly in their books by saying:

Take that which is closest to nature; from that draw our Stone, etc. And I have revealed to you all the things the Philosophers have kept secret. My child must know that this precious Stone is prepated in many different ways. This Stone can be used for any works one wishes, for it is now ready to receive whatever spiritus or soul one adds to it, either for the Medicine or for Alchymy. Ths Stone is not a chooser of persons, for it accepts everything one adds to it, either for the Medicine or for

Alchymy. This Stone is not a chooser of persons, for it accepts everything one adds to it; for it is fixed and dry to the fourth degree, also cold, and all spiritus are volatile, hot and humid. That is why all spirits desire to be with this Stone; and that is the reason why some philosophers have called this Stone the Son of God, for He was no respecter of persons.

Item, the old sages have brought this Stone back to its first nature and utmost perfection. As they say: Four things arise from one thing. That is to say, the old people sought one thing and one root out of which four things originate. And when they were able to convert them back into one thing, the QE was achieved, valid in all eternity.

I know of no thing in the whole world which would be as good and wholesome to our nature as this divine Stone of the philosophers.

Now we will again give information on how we are to prepare our Stone, which is at first a dead corpus but has been glorified and made pure, and suitable to set in it the spirit of life and the perfect soul and to make them eternal.

If you wish to make this Stone come alive, you may bring it to any body you wish. You can make of it a Lapis Philosophorum or QE, which cure all sicknesses, which sustain man's body in full health and let him last without decrease of the body in full health and let him last without decrease of the body till the last termin of everybody's life, as we heard above. But if you wish to make of it a medicine for unclean metals, you must take it to metals, for a horse makes a horse, etc.

Further, then, in order to achieve our purpose, my child should take * dissolved AF, sublimate it 4 or 5 times through vitriol and salt. The more it is sublimated, the greater will its projection be. Following this, Mercury thus sublimated is to be rubbed to a powder on a stone, and this is to be put into a wide vessel, one thumb thick. Set it in tripode to calcinate for 8 days, however only with a gentle coal fire, so that you can keep your hand over the fire for the length of an Ave Maria.

Now take it out and dissolve it in Aquafort made of saltpetre 1 part, vitriol Romani 2 parts, cinnabar 1/2 part, * 1/4 part. From this make AF, as you know, and rectify it as it should, etc. Then dissolve as many z Sol as you have pounds of Mercury; dissolve each in a separate glass, and when Mercury and Sol are dissolved, pour the two waters together and set them in the Balneum. Let them stand of 7 days to unite, that is, the spiritus and the soul. Then all three will turn into water; let them stand dissolved into water for 3 or 4 days, so that they may become well united and marry each other; and five more spiritus than you have corporis or stones, because the corpus will not absorb more spiritus that it has a right to. Now distill the water per alembicum out of the Balneum. Pulverize them on a stone, put them into a wide vessel, one thumb thick, set the vessel in Tripode to digest and to calcinate for 8 days and nights, with a moderate fire. Then take it out, put the matter into a glass pot, lute a small glass on the mouth of the pot, and set it to sublimate, since I have taught you before that you should take much more spiritus than you have corporis, and in this sublimation the corpus will let the spiritus of which it has too much, go.

Let it stand in the pot for 3 days and nights with a good life as is necessary for sublimation. Then take the pot down and take the Stone out. Test it on a copper, glowing sheet; see if it melts like wax, spreading on the sheet, penetrating into it like fat into dry leather. See if after the sheet has cooled down the spot where the Stone has spread is good gold in all tests --- then your Stone is valuable and all ready and accomplished.

But if it is not, you must dissolve it again in the AF and set it again into the Balneum Mariae, 7 days. After this, again conceal it, and take it out again. And let it stand once again in Tripode for 8 days, as before. Then take it out, test it as before, and the more you dissolve and congeal it, the greater will be its projection. If the Stone does one to a hundred, and you dissolve and congeal it again it will make a ten times higher projection. But I advise you to do it but 3 times, because the Stone would reach such great power and subtlety that it could not be kept in any kind of vessel. That is how penetrating it is said to be.

Consequently, I advise you to dissolve and congeal and calcinate it in tripode only 3 times. Then the Stone will become subtle and strong of its own, so much so that it is unbelievable. If gold is put into some oil, no one can express the abundance of its color. Yes, then it is of such great potency that if a man were to put 3 drops of oleum solis into a little rectified aqua vitae, he would retain his youth to the last days of his life as it is ordained for him. Bu this kind of oil must be made quite differently, not like the ordinary oil, which is made with AF. The oleum solis, however, which is prepared as a medicine for the human body, is made of two elements which you must draw from our Stone, that is, the elements air and fire. With these you must prepare your gold oil.

Take gold, beaten thinly like gold leaves between paper, and rub it on a stone with distilled wine vinegar or with some water of * or of the element which you have drawn from our Stone. When it is powdered finely, put it into a glass pot. Into the same pot put the element which you have drawn out of our Stone. Cover the pot and set it on sand for 3 or 4 days. After that, open it, and you will find your gold transformed into an oil. Distill the element from it, and in fundo you will find a golden oil. That is the greatest medicine one can find in the world.

Another Method Which Is Easier

Take our Stone in its coarseness such as it comes out of the minera of man. Understand well what I am saying! Put it into a wide, glass vessel and add the powdered gold leaves. Pour on this some of our Stone, which must be old and well settled and purified. Pour of the Stone, two fingers; width over the gold. Set the vessel with gold and the Stone of summer into the heat of the sun. A white-golden skin or oil will form on top. Remove it carefully with a feather, in such a way that you move the matter as little as possible. Put it ninto a glass. Proceed in this way several times a day, removing the oil till no more oil forms on top. Thus you can obtain oleum solis with our Stone in its coarseness, as it comes out of a man's minera.

Understand well what I have hinted at here, because there has never been a greater secret in nature concerning our Stone, which also, in spite of its coarseness, transforms gold into oil. And very many artists have sought this secret but have not found it. Therefore, be grateful to God, etc. If then this our Stone accomplishes this in its crude stage, just imagine what it will do when it is perfected and united with the spirit and soul, and is fixed subtle and fusible. Do ponder over my words, so that you do not do useless work.

Now we will again resolve to prepare our Stone for such great strength that it is unbelievable. You must therefore continue to dissolve the Stone in the water of the Hand, as I have taught you above. Dissolve and coagulate, and then calcine it in Tripode as before. Do this three times and no more. Otherwise it would become all too penetrating and strong, as described above.

If, however, you wish to have your Stone augmented and multiplied, say one to a thousand, take 10 lbs of fie gold or silver. After having prepared your Stone as before, melt it on fire in a crucible. After this, throw 1 lb of your Stone on it, and let them flow together strongly for a good half hour. Now pour it into a pewter vessel, or let it cool down of its own. Your gold and silver will be brittle or crumbly, since too much medicine has been put on it. For this is the test of the elixirs: If one wishes to make projection with a certain thing, and one does not really know the projection, one throws the medicine on any metal one chooses. As long as the metal stays brittle, the medicine will accomplish yet higher projections. Now throw the brittle metal upon other metals, till the metals stay subtle, etc. Keep this, for this is the end of the projection.

I said, you should throw 1 lb of the Stone on 10 lbs of gold or silver, according to what kind of soul your Stone has, since your Stone is supposed to operate on unclean metals; 1 lb to 1000 lbs for good gold. And I instructed you to throw it on 10 lbs of gold or silver. But this is done so that the 10 lbs of gold or silver should also turn into medicine, because gold or silver does not require any medicine; but they will turn into a medicine which is better than your Stone. The reason is that while the stone which you have thrown upon them is in itself the soul of the gold or the silver, the gold or silver is medicinated. It is now a medicine and brittle like your Stone.

Pulverize the gold or silver there is, and dissolve it in the water of the Hand which is used for the White or the Red, etc. Set it to putrefy into the balneum for 7 days. Then abstract the water per alembicum, and congeal the matter. Remove it, pulverize it intangibly on a stone, and put it into a wide vessel of one thumb's thickness. Keep it in Tripode for 8 days with a moderate fire, somewhat hotter. Do this, dissolving, congealing, and calcining in Tripode, three times, and your matter will be stronger and better than your Stone. The reason is that your Stone is the soul of your matter, and the gold is the corpus of the souls. When the gold has been turned into oil, it has a hundred times more power, as said above.

Gold, however, is not just oil but also a medicine, just as good as is the Stone. Example: give poison to someone, as big as a bean, an evil, strong poison. That man will die immediately, because the poison courses to the heart and through all arteries, including all flesh and the whole abdomen. It poisons the whole body. And f a man were to eat of an animal to which the poison has been given, as I have here described, all those who had eaten of it would die. It is possible therefore, to give to a man or an animal, poison the size of a bean, so that the whole body would become poisonous --- all those who would eat of it would die. What should you now think of gold or silver? And even if gold or silver were not medicated but only amalgamated precipitation in their raw state with Mercury, and they were kept together in moderate fire, do you not think that the gold or silver would change mercury into its nature? Yes, certainly, and that in a short time, within four weeks.

If then the gold and silver (even in their raw state) can bring about the change of Mercury into their own nature, what will they do when they are medicinated with the noblest medicine of the world and are applied so abundantly? Such medicinated gold or silver is also dissolved in the water of the Hand, kept in Balneo for 7 days and nights in order to digest. Afterwards it is again congealed and then calcined in Tripode, and this is done three times. What do you think of that? And even if they had not been medicinated but had by themselves been calcined and congealed, would it not have made a medicine all of itself? Indeed, yes. If you have intelligence, understand my words. If you do not understand, you are an oaf. I have here taught you how to make the most precious of them most unprecious. Thank God Almighty that you have got this instruction.

End of the Work of the Stone of Urine.

Here Begins the Other Way of Alchemy

This has been mentioned before and it is an: Elixir

Now we will deal with the second way of alchymy, that is, how to make an Elixir, just as our ancestors have left is and had made themselves, as I have also worked it with my own hands.

First it is necessary to convert all things into water before they can be used or applied in our Art, as Aristotle says in the Book of Secrets. I do not believe that one thing can be changed into its nature unless it be first brought back into the nature in which it had been originally made. And when it has been brought back into its first nature, then I believe, says Aristotle, that the thing can be changed into any nature one wishes. As all things originally arose from one water, one cannot do otherwise than turn them back into water before allowing them to play their part in the Art. Therefore, you must first change all Spirits into water before sublimating them, or else you will never reach perfection.

Likewise, anything by which you sublimate the Spirits must also first be converted into water. If not, the work is totally lost. Therefore, first turn Mercury into water with Aquafort. Then it will discard its faeces, its coldness will be changed into heat, and its moisture into dryness. Its color will also be increased, since it is the nature of Mercury to absorb the QE, and at the same time, it will also become a QE because mercury is QE and you can perfectly extract four elements from mercury. Consequently, one has to first dissolve Mercury in AF before sublimating it, and such a sublimation makes Mercury and all other spirits dry, hot and subtle because its power is augmented tenfold with every sublimation. Note: this is to be understood by sublimation: Sublimate Mercury only once, and make an elixir of it. Then it will not do more than 1 opn 10. But if you sublimate it 10 times, and then make an elixir of it, it will do 1 on 100.

After it has been sublimated, it must first calcined because Mercury contains volatile Spirits which could never be fixed. Those Spirits disappear with a calcinations in Tripode. If they were not driven away, you could never achieve a fixation with Mercury.

Furthermore, when Mercury has been calcined, it must then be dissolved in aquafort and poured off from its faeces because it accumulates dust and impurities during calcinations. If you now wish to make it subtle, purify it in the Balneum and congeal it. After that, sublimate it again, and in the sublimation, you will find 20 while at first you only found 10. Dissolve this sublimated Mercury again in AD, as much as you wish. But now it must not again be calcined in Tripode as it no longer contains any volatile Spirits. You could sublimate and dissolve Mercury so often and render it so subtle that it is absolutely marvelous since it is sublimated through Roman Vitriol, from which it takes all the tinctures which the AF contains.

Now we will further speak of what is to be done with gold and silver before they are added to their Spirits and Bodies. Gold or silver must be purified on the test or through cementation. Now dissolve it in AF and decant it from its faeces. Distill the AF off from it in a lukewarm BM. Pour on fresh AF, close the glass tightly, seal it and put it back in the BM. In the meantime, the Soul of the gold will become so subtle that it will thereafter never again become a body. Now the AF has to again be drawn off in a lukewarm BM and the material has to be set in Tripode in a closed vessel for 6 weeks. The fire must be half stronger than it was when the Spirits were calcined. The gold or silver is made so subtle that it is unbelievable, and the projection will be infinite.

In addition, we will show what has to be done with the Bodies, that is, with our Stone. After we have made it clear and subtle, it is required that it be dissolved in AF, and set in the BM, well sealed, to putrefy for as long as we wish, but the longer the better. The stronger and more powerful it becomes, the higher will be the projection.

Further, we will show, how are we to collect the Spirit, Soul and Body, conjoin them, with the help of God Almighty, marry, fix and perfect them; likewise how this projection is to be made, etc. First, it is necessary to dissolve the Body or Stone in AF. Then it has to putrefy for at least 7 days in BM, unless you wish to prepare it differently from what I have taught above. You should at least purify your gold or silver on the test or in cement. Thereafter dissolve it in aquafort, whereby gold is separated from silver. That is common separation water. Proceed likewise with your silver and set it in BM to putrefy. Always close you vessels well before setting them in BM. Your sublimated Mercury must likewise be dissolved in aquafort, kept in BM for 7 days and nights. Each (gold, silver, mercury) must be treated separately. When they are thus putrefied and dissolved, let all three substances cool. Take a big glass pot and put them into it. If now you have gold, which is your Soul, the waters will not become impure, but if it is silver, they will become troubled on account of the Body, as it contains some saltiness, and it will precipitate as if it were milk curd. Now put an alembic on it and distill the moisture from it in the BM with a gentle fire. But if the congealed mass does not dissolve after you have poured fresh good aquafort on it, do it once more, as I taught you before, and, if necessary, a third time. Then it will without doubt, dissolve into clear water. When it is dissolved, let it stand in BM for 7 days.

Now take cupel silver that has been cemented or calcined once or twice in prepared salt, then changed back into a Body. Laminate that silver and cut it into pieces, as small as possible. Keep throwing one of these little pieces into the material, till the latter no longer dissolves the silver but leaves it whole. Then it is enough. Now congeal your material. And as I wrote about silver, do likewise with the gold, but the latter will not become turbid at the bottom. When you now bring these three waters together, you must once or twice draw the water over from the gold in the BM. Again, pour AF on it and proceed further as with the silver. If you do not find it fusible enough, calcine it once more in AF and simultaneously dissolve sulfur that has been sublimated 4 or 5 times. Keep it in the BM until your

Stone and Sulhpur are dissolved into a water. Then congeal this wit a gentle fire, and your Stone will be fusible enough and is now ready to be used for projection.

I did this work once myself and found it to be good. The same work can be done in different ways. All these works ended well but there was a great difference in the projection which varied according to the manner in which the works had been undertaken and the Soul, Spirit and Body had been prepared. It was always good gold or silver in all assays but not in the works, because the gold and silver therin are too even, although they both passed all tests. But the gold which is so wonderfully prepared for tinctures and made subtle, must be of a higher and better quality --- which is self-evident.

Likewise for silver made of tin. It is much more beautiful in color than that made of copper, because copper is closer to gold than to silver. But whoever wants to make a projection with Ixirs falls on no other metals than copper only. The reason is the following: Venus is easier to transmute from one nature to another than any of the other metals. There are no metals in nature that are so closely perfected toward gold or silver than copper. Therefore, if you wish to make a projection with the Ixir, whereby our stone is not prepared --- it is necessary first to dissolve copper in AF, then to reduce it again into a Body. If you wish to make a projection on it, then melt the copper and add to every pound of copper one quarter pound of fine silver. After that, throw the Ixir on it, and the silver will become all the more beautiful and white. The copper made with the Ixir from copper is harder to work with, forge, and melt than the silver prepared with a perfected elixir. Then, when thrown on tin, it is so malleable and easy to work with that all who handle it are amazed at it. Therefore, you must know how to distinguish silver transmuted by an Ixir from that transmuted by an Elixir.

End of the Second Way of Alchemy.

The Third Way of Alchemy Called : Ixir.

Now I will continue with a few words on the Ixir, which is the third piece of work on which Alchymy is based, as I mentioned in the beginning of this book. You must know that one can well make an Ixir with our Stone, for where the Soul, Spirit and Body are not duly joined together, nor are congealed together, they are called Ixirs that are not perfected. But where the Soul, Body and Spirit are duly joined and congealed together, and have also been made fusible, they are Elixirs and good throughout all eternity.

The Elixir transmutes all impure metals into fine gold and silver, without any help from other things. I advise you, however, not to undertake any projection on Venus with an Elixir, but only on the best and most yellow brass, as the Elixir will then achieve a much higher projection than on either Jupiter or red copper. Furthermore, they will be all the more beautiful and striking because you will then have the advantage of the colors. But with the Ixir, no projection can be made except on the metal of Venus alone. And, if you had a white Ixir, it would be necessary first to make the Venus white with soft waters, after calcining it. In any event, you must take calcinated brass before throwing your Ixir on it, otherwise you will be in error and go wrong. Take good heed of this.

End of the Third Way of Alchymy.

www.ingramcontent.com/pod-product-compliance
Lightning Source LLC
Chambersburg PA
CBHW060504110426
42738CB00055B/2673